Fix That Bell!

by Becca Heddle
Illustrated by Bill Ledger

OXFORD
UNIVERSITY PRESS

In this story ...

Ben

Ben can run as fast as a truck.

Pip

Mrs Butterworth

Magnus

The lunch bell rings.

Ben is peckish.

We must dash!

Ben gets fish and chips with a drink.

Just then, the bell rings.

The bell rings and rings.

I will get Magnus.

Magnus pulls the top off the bell.

ping

The springs drop.

Ben rushes to get the springs.

I will get them.

Magnus fixes the bell.

Ben sits, but then the bell rings!
It is the end of lunch.

Magnus hands Ben a sandwich and a drink.

Retell the story ...

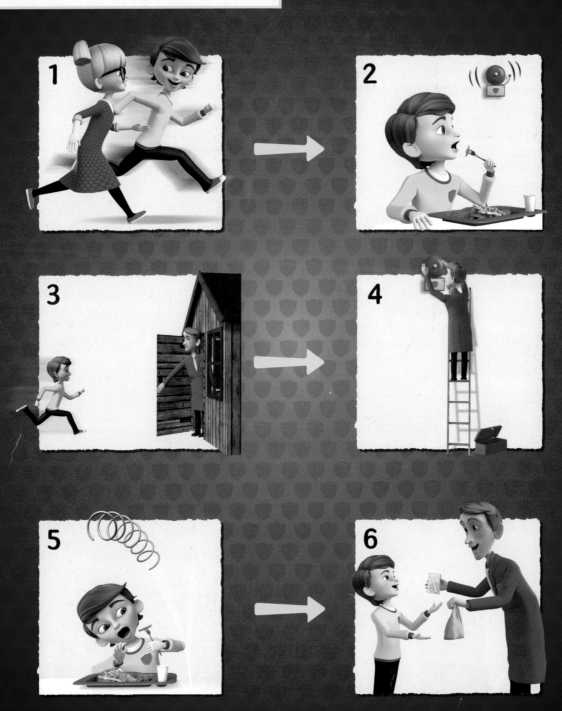